Conspire To Inspire

Thoughts Matter

Umaima Vaziri

Made with ❤ on the BookLeaf Publishing Platform
www.bookleafpub.in
www.bookleafpub.com

Dedication

"To my faith, which grounds me in every word I write,
To my parents, for their unwavering love and guidance,
To my husband, for his constant support,
And to my children, who inspire me."

Preface

"The more you observe, the more you are in awe. God's creation is just perfect—there is no place for a flaw."

I began writing when I was 14 years old—not to become a poet, but simply to release the thoughts that swirled in my mind. For over a decade, I have used poetry as a way to express the moments of my life that I couldn't otherwise articulate. It became more than just words—it was art to me. Poetry was a mirror of my mind, a way to release tension, and a medium for the conversations I couldn't have aloud. It's a form of self-expression that allowed me to speak to myself, the world, and those I love.

This collection, *Conspire to Inspire: Thoughts Matter*, is a reflection of that journey. Each poem is a piece of my life, offering food for thought through simplicity. While there is no singular theme binding these poems, the overarching idea is that our thoughts matter. They are substantial, designed to shape our experiences and influence how we live our lives. Through these words, I hope to inspire others to think beyond their immediate reality and open their hearts to love more deeply.

Writing, for me, has always been a way to understand the world. It's a gift I've inherited, a way to connect to those around me. The thoughts and experiences shared in these poems are shaped by the profound impact of my family—my grandmother, whose poetic talent lives on in me; my parents, who gently guided and supported me through every walk of life; and my teacher, who helped shape the person I am today. Writing is a gift I've been fortunate enough to inherit, and now, I would like to share it with you.

This collection is a reflection of my belief that, as humans, we must always strive to better ourselves and, in doing so, inspire others to do the same. *Conspire to Inspire*—together, we can make the world a better place, one thought at a time.

Acknowledgements

1. Conspire to Inspire

Conspire to inspire,
Inspire to admire,
Admire to aspire,
Aspire to set fire
To your demons
That conspire.

Note: *To be an inspiration, one must first strive, work hard, and embody goodness, reaching a place where others can look up to them. But true elevation comes when the inspiration shifts inward—recognizing the vastness of the world and admiring the greatness beyond the self. In this space of admiration, we realize that the greatest challenge and victory lie in overcoming our own demons. Through self-reflection and continuous betterment, we find the strength to inspire once more.*

2. Thoughts

What is the limit?
That a thought could reach,
If it could float away from my mind?
I have heard
that thoughts can weigh,
They are substantial, they are defined.
It seems they have power.
Thoughts could make Reality!
You can call them magical or
just well designed.

Notes: *Our mind is the core of our being, hidden from the world and known only to us and our Creator. This makes it one of our most valuable gifts. Our thoughts have weight—they shape our perception define who we are, giving us the power to design our existence.*

3. Contentment

Pause.
Breathe.
Hope.
See.
Release the mind.
Shed the load.
Slow down.
Rewind.
Sit back.
Intertwine.
Earn your keep.
Yearn for peace.
Contentment—
A place,
A balance,
An emotion.
A stillness that frees.

Note: *To connect with oneself and attain freedom, contentment is essential. It is a sense of peace, a stillness within. By pausing the clutter of thoughts, slowing down, and finding balance, we reach a place where our emotions reassure us that we are in the best place we can be.*

4. If a Pen Could...

If a pen could relay all my thoughts,
All those tiny speckles and threads that get often lost,
My eye would describe the finest details,
And my hand would draw all its artistic tales.
If my heart could reveal what it thinks,
All those flutters and its strongest strings,
My beats would tell those thoughts to share,
And my touch would make the world stop and stare.

Notes: *Sometimes, we struggle to express ourselves—*
We fumble, we trip, and we slip.
The feelings we hold and the thoughts we think,
We often fail to let them sink.
But I know, when those emotions break free,
In any form they take, they'll become a masterpiece.
And when they pour out, raw and true,
The world will have no choice but to acknowledge you—
For simply being you.

5. The Narration

A book
Turns its pages
With a soft, gentle stir.
The flip of the edges,
And the sounds that murmur.
The stories
Unfold their mysteries,
Reciting the weight of their words.
The stops and the lapses
Add intrigue to their worlds.
The end,
Likes to be chased down
By overzealous beginnings,
The length of the passage
Tells the story of the innings.

Note: *Our lives whisper softly, creating ripples that often go unnoticed. The journey may feel slow, but it's the moments in between—the pauses, turns, and steps—that shape our story. These fleeting moments hold our true essence, leaving an imprint that never fades.*

6. We Can Just Mimic!

When we mimic nature,
Using our skills,
It is in the nature of nature
To bloom everywhere
It instills.

Note: *The best way to grow is to learn, and what better teacher than — nature? why do we sometimes overlook the wisdom that surrounds us?*

7. Sailing the Horizon

The places we cherish,
The moments in those,
The people we share it,
Whose doors are never closed.

The horizon is what we choose—
It could be a mile, it could be a pool.
Bringing light into darkness
Can be one's greatest tool.

Sailing has never been easy;
The wind takes its share.
Being steady in all weathers,
Is a drift so fair and rare.

Note: *Can we remain steady and weather the storm?*
Can we sail toward the horizon and smile all along?

8. Horizon

When I look across the horizon,
Through the beauty of the muddled illusion,
Even a puddle of water -
appears like the never-ending ocean.

Note: *Maybe what we feel is just an illusion. Sometimes, we must give reality the chance to unveil itself.*

9. Her Reach

Reaching out for great things,
Even when they are far,
Your hands might be small,
But your mind has no bar.

Seeking out rare things,
Maybe as bright as a star.
Your eyes may be keen,
But it might be better afar.

Note: *Reaching for great things, even when they seem distant. Despite physical limitations, the mind knows no bounds. Sometimes, the pursuit of greatness is best admired from afar.*

10. It is You for You!

It does not matter to the world
who you are
or
what you have **done**.

There will always be someone
to take your place,
no matter
what you have **won**.

It does not matter to the world
what you are made of.
If
you do not do it for yourself,
it matters to no **one**.

Not even Einstein or Bill Gates
or
any other man with a million traits
could keep a pedestal for too long—
it is the way it **is**.

If you keep quiet and fade away,
it is **you**

who will be wasted,
it is **you**
who will lose your **say**.

It is
the reality of this world.
The wheels of destiny
are at play.

It is
just you for you.
Bend low,
and have it all your way.

Note: *Even selflessness earns its own reward—respect. In a world where righteousness often seeks validation, true humility remains a poem of its own.*

11. Well, Vain, Still

It may all be meant well,
Your love and caring engraved deep within.
Your thoughts sure and your soul pure,
All your achievements, negation of sin.

It may all be in vain,
If your actions are short of what's within.
A wrong word, emotions stirred,
All that was earned will be sent to the bin.

It may all be fine still,
Understanding and empathy build it within.
Do for others, be kind, dear brothers.
Let the heart be an ocean; someday you will win.

Note: *I wish we could all have hearts as big as the ocean. My dad taught me that... I wish I could always remember that.*

12. When You Were Told

Those days when you were told,
"These are the best, better **behold**."

Those days when you were told,
"Learn the best, make yourself **unfold**."

Those days when you were told,
"You are the best, be strong and **bold**."

Those days when you were told,
"Take your rest, shelter from hot and **cold**."

Those days when you were told,
"Do not test, patience is **gold**."

Those days when you were told,
"It is not a jest, you will grow **old**."

Note: *"Do not make the mistake of thinking you're above advice, because one day, you'll grow old, and one day, you'll understand what you had been told."*

13. My Lost Laughter

Once upon a time,
I lost my laughter.
I searched everywhere,
Here and there,
Hoping to go and get her.
Stretching my thoughts wide,
Looking at every side,
With sadness in my eyes,
I went back to find her.
I realized what I missed—
Every second that I risked
Without her.
I didn't find her here,
I didn't find her there,
But I found her everywhere.
I heard her—
Laughter in the air.
That makes it fair,
So everyone can have her.
So I looked back inside,
And found her beside,
Right where I lost her.
Note: Sometimes, we search for joy in all the wrong places, not realizing it was within us all along.

14. Is Love Like the Beanstalk?

My love is stronger than the beanstalk,
And much taller for you to gawk.
There are many hidden treasures,
Beware! Words will be short for you to talk.

There could be giants and geese,
Harmoniums that say peace,
Golden eggs and long legs,
And food to make you obese.

A castle in the clouds,
A huge door and many sounds,
A kind-hearted giant's wife,
With treats unseen in your life.

Don't be greedy, that's the law,
Or you will be chased down this flaw.
You will cut the bloke at the bend,
We don't want to see such an awful end.

Many things written above
May make no sense to you, my love.
The beanstalk just fascinates me,
Have a laugh, but it isn't stupidity.

It says a lot, you might not know,
Infatuation is not love when you sow.
The gleams may fade, and the dangers may show,
It will bring pain, no matter how you let it grow.

Good night, have pleasant dreams.
Enjoy your fantasies under the moonlight beams.
May no giant disturb you there,
May you sleep with love and care.

Note: *"It happens to be"*

15. Labyrinth

A labyrinth is enjoyable when you know there is a way
out.
Its colors are enticing when you know they will fade out.
The glamour might intoxicate,
The novelty might instigate,
But as time passes,
The colors, the glamour, the novelty of it start to
suffocate.

Note: *Understanding the path that should not be taken is
more valuable than knowing the path that should be.*

16. The Sound of - The Cry

Once upon a time,
There was the sound of a cry—
A cry that made them smile,
With tears in their eyes.

Once upon a time,
There was a movement like a smile—
A smile that sent their world twirling
For a while.

Once upon a time,
There were long nights like days—
Days that turned into nights
In countless ways.

And the story went on—
Their adventure of life was born,
Born around this joy
That they lovingly adorn.

Years passed, yet they carried on—
Selfless, wise, and never torn.
Their every breath was meant to teach,
A courage to lean upon.

Then came a time—the hourglass turned,
The cry was heard again.
Once more, with those tears, came that smile,
And realization struck—so plain.

Note: *No matter what anyone tells you, some things can only be understood through experience.*

17. Heavy - Transitory

"When the gloom weighs down heavy,
Your presence becomes my story.
Your love, my shining glory—
Everything else feels transitory."

Note: *When life's weight feels unbearable, it's the love and presence of those who matter that bring light and meaning, reminding us that everything else is temporary.*

18. The Kid Effect!

Kids have a way of creeping
In your heart and seeping—
Love in your soul,
And bringing joy and brightness
Like never before.
They teach us how to love and adore,
They make us appreciate life even more.

Note: *"Observe those little hearts—they are much more than we think they are."*

19. Will Happen Anyway

He got up one morning,
All charged up for the day—
A long to-do list,
And passion in his mind lay.
A belief in his talents,
Strong in his ways,
To capture the world,
To provide value that pays.
To reach the stars was his aim.
Work hard he did, never lay.
His time was too precious—
Successful he was, some may say.
He thought the world needed him,
That things wouldn't work night and day.
There were very few
To take his place in a way.
But the world has its course,
Its plan, its surreal own ways.
Things bound to happen
Will happen anyway.
The stars will shift,
The oceans will drift,
The air will greet,
The sun will beat.

The things bound to happen
Will happen anyway.

Note: *"Things bound to happen, happen anyway. Your greatness is a gift—don't let it make you sway."*

20. Social Pause

I am not social,
I am scarce.
I don't need to show up,
If my heart does not ask.

I am not available,
I am not a farce.
I don't need attention,
At least, not from the vast.

I say I don't care—
I say it again,
again, and again,
Until it feels like a mask.

No need to follow,
No need to like,
I can grow, I can flow,
I can be a social dislike.

My talent is mine,
Its whispers are mine,
For me, for me,
For me is the rhyme.

You can leave me,
You can, you can,
Leave me, you can—
But I'll still love the best I can.

I'll love the best I can.

Note: *Sometimes, pausing and building yourself—nurturing your ability to love—is more important than paying attention to what others are doing. It's not a race with the world, but with yourself.*

21. Shadows glorify

Uncovering the True Beauty of Our Story
In an unusual way,
Just like sunlight lighting up a glorious day,
Making patterns with the help of shadows' play.
Shadows have their own ways.
Shadows glorify those pretty rays.

Note: *Would light be as beautiful if shadows didn't exist?*

22. Happiness Blooms from Pain

With all the troubles that surround,
A pattern unfolds all around.
At the point when it all weighs down,
You can hear your breath drown.

Then, isn't life about suffering?
Even happiness arrives blustering.
Fulfilling expectations—is it just a fantasy?
We hold on to wants, not thought through rationally.

This world is a field of alchemy.
It's in your hands to not let pain turn into tragedy,
But in HIS hands to turn affliction into purity—
In ways you cannot perceive, so let's thank for eternity.

NOTE: *"If pain is a necessary part of transformation, could your struggles be shaping something greater within you?"*

23. At the Roadside Café!

Imagine...
A cold, windy day.
Your palms are shivering
Under the gloves you wear.
With you are your loved ones,
Laughing with play.
You sit down on those chairs,
Chatting away...
Or maybe waiting for someone
Who has lost their way.
You look around and smile,
You've had a wonderful day.
Maybe you drink coffee
To keep the chill at bay.
You click a photo
To remember someday...
To remember someday...

Note: *Life's simple moments, that you want to freeze into your memory.*
Because they evoke such warmth that you cannot just forget, they are nostalgic, and poetic.

24. Opinions

Opinions are so easy to form,
They are like berry picking on a farm.
And sometimes they fly like pollen
And land like an unexpected swarm.
You might not like the berries,
You might not like their zest,
But still, picking them
Feels like a treasure chest.

Once they are in your basket,
They are your very own.
You might add your own sugar
And share it with some unknown.
While sharing is thoughtful,
It has its benefits,
But be prudent in what you give—
It may be beyond clever wits.

It is possible they might harm,
Like the fact of varied taste buds.
It is possible they don't always charm.
Berries from another's basket
Might seem very nice,
But if you have too many,
Collecting more might not be wise.

Weigh your basket not once, maybe thrice.
Keep your berries with you,
That is the best way to summarize.

Note: *Are all berries worth picking?*

25. Looking Back

Looking back at another year,
Being thankful for things far and near.
The horizon has never been this bright,
A sea of love brimming with glorious light.
Looking back at another year,
Grateful for things small and dear.
Possibilities like soft molding sand,
Hope of adventures crossing sea and land.

Note: *Dreaming of making realities—where hope meets action, possibilities take shape, and gratitude paves the way.*

26. The Significance of Being Insignificant

If I contemplate weighing a grain of sand
Against the vast expanse of the universe,
Will that grain not exist?
If that grain does not exist,
Can the universe exist?
Maybe we got it all backwards.
**"Maybe being insignificant
Holds the most significance."**